your beating heart
)that beating heart(
is the greatest sound
is the greatest elixir
is the greatest wonder
that astonishes
that validates
that sparks
all reasons
to smile wider
to treat better
to love louder
to exist fuller
to fill deeper
and
always
always
always
cherish each day
each moment
and bloom
into beautiful magic.

xo. adrian michael

xo.lvst.

books by adrian michael

loamexpressions

blinking cursor

notes of a denver native son

blackmagic

lovehues

notes from a gentle man

blooming hearts

book of her book of she

for hearts that ache.

he was taught to be this way. I + II

giver. I + II + III

love hopes for you. I + II + III

xo.lvst.

words you didn't know you needed to hear.

xo.lvst.

adrian michael

a lovasté project
in partnership with hwttbtw
published by
creative genius
CONCORDHAUS

Published by Creative Genius Publishing—
an imprint of lovasté

| Denver, CO | Concord, CA |

To contact the author:
    visit adrianmichaelgreen.com
To see more of the author's work:
    visit IG @adrianmichaelgreen
Book jacket designed by Adrian Michael Green

ISBN-13: 9798730397361

Printed in the United States of America

for you.
always for you.

adore you x harry styles
what you want x jvck james
i get to love you x ruelle
everything x ella mai + john legend
by your side x sade
conversations in the dark x john legend
before you go x lewis capaldi
leave the door open x bruno mars + anderson .paak
grow as we go x ben platt
ribbon in the sky x stevie wonder
i do x alo blacc + leann rimes
if you're tired x connor duermit + ray dalton
pillowtalk x zayn
all to me x giveon
butterflies x james tw
good thing x maple gilder
roll some mo x lucky daye + chronixx + medisun
cruisin' x smokey robinson
when you love someone x tone stith + h.e.r.
you x triathalon
come thru x summer walker + usher
little wing x jimi hendrix
summertime magic x childish gambino
want u around x omar apollo + ruel
tell me you love me x demi lovato
wildfire x cautious clay

incense. palo santo. candles. sage.
tea. whiskey. wine. water. beer.

a well full of water.	1
meeting you wasn't the destination.	2
unable to think straight.	3
i watched a ripple once.	4
soul treasure.	5
the artist.	6
tangled.	7
you have the right to remain original.	8
full of grace that feeds my sin.	9
social security numbers.	10
where love was first discovered.	11
the gasps between each breath.	12
i used to close my eyes under water.	13
love is a dedication page.	14
each day something beautiful happens.	15
heartbeat trembling.	16
exotic expression.	17
in the dark.	18
you breathe life.	19
not just anyone can stand that much heat.	20
you always find a way.	21
i love you.	22
the story of you.	23
every bit of you.	24
laughter is love.	25
burning point.	26
airwaves.	27
amor on glass.	28
you are magic.	29
the souls way.	30
why read a book on love.	31

love is.	32
inferno.	33
sorry if i stare.	34
moments.	35
acoustic bliss.	36
water.	37
soak me up.	38
you blot the sky.	39
the echo of your heartbeat.	40
the honey on your bones.	41
searching.	42
looking for aurora.	43
forgetting to breathe.	44
sky love.	45
fine art.	46
i'll lay.	47
nothing fiction about you.	48
euphoric bliss.	49
definition.	50
tragedy.	51
an odd prayer.	52
they want it all from you.	53
russian roulette.	54
on my lips i carry your name.	55
magic heartbeats.	56
cosmic rendezvous.	57
waiting for your return.	58
admire just admire.	59
favorite wrinkle.	60
ode to you.	61
crème glacée.	62

take life as it comes.	63
the masks we wear.	64
fixated light.	65
what if what if.	66
i see you.	67
love currency.	68
flirting eyes.	69
tiles.	70
don't flee.	71
north star.	72
becoming my gravity.	73
the hare has always been me.	74
insatiable.	75
fingerprints on my soul.	76
you bewitched the world.	77
everything about you.	78
the key ingredient.	79
bring back our girls.	80
you broke my levees.	81
compliments.	82
the shoes in the corner.	83
i can't give you flowers.	84
breathing you in.	85
making you ring.	86
love territory.	87
will you be my.	88
in a gallery on display.	89
on a crusade for words.	90
i see time by looking into your eyes.	91
stargazing.	92
for the one who is kind is beautiful.	93

you are you. 94

like braille. 95

your accent. 96

your love is magic i believe in. 97

before you or i ever existed. 98

passport kisses. 99

midnight moon. 100

an imperfect host. 101

;. 102

everything to you is a fire. 103

look at me look at you. 104

the octaves of your voice. 105

nostalgic souls. 106

love is light. 107

don't put out the light. 108

love magic. 109

tenderness to mend a broken heart. 110

this love thing. 111

why this infatuation with the stars. 112

you aren't broken. 113

worry worry. 114

you have consumed my soul. 115

being with you. 116

the pull of you. 117

give me nothing. 118

the sum of all of you. 119

i have studied your lips. 120

make our own atmosphere. 121

your skin is a wonder of the world. 122

love is a mountain. 123

the universe belongs to you. 124

let the waters find their way.	125
utter madness the things i'd do for you.	126
let me become these words.	127
eclipse.	128
up close.	129
may there be more of you.	130
shake.	131
back to life.	132
the bubbles we make.	133
en la distancia.	134
worth losing track of.	135
on my walk home.	136
a note to you.	137
if i had one word left to say.	138
freckles.	139
the forever hello.	140
they don't know poetry.	141
thank you for us.	142
the greatest rays.	143
never had the courage but i do now.	144
smiling looks good on you.	145
the lover in me honors the lover in you.	146
piece in peace.	147
our title don't matter.	148
lost and found.	149
lift me to your atmosphere.	150
mighty sol.	151
burst like a butterfly from its cocoon.	152
the vows we never wrote.	153
i'll never play for your heart.	154
xo.lvst.	155

a well full of water.

i looked into your eyes
and finally saw you.

a well full of water
not wanting to be saved

but to be
understood.

meeting you wasn't the destination.

meeting you wasn't the destination
simply the beginning of a beautiful journey
where souls collide and twirl.

unable to think straight.

i never know
never know what to say
not due to lack of words
)i have a slew of those(
but because)i'll admit(
you fill my veins
every single one
and before i know it
my brain is intoxicated
unable to think straight.

i watched a ripple once.

i watched a ripple once
and the dimples it made
in the stillness of water
echoed heavily
in my soul

you
are
the ringlets
in my sea.

soul treasure.

ribs
aren't
cages
they
are
gates
to
your
castle
the
drawbridge
to
soul
treasure.

the artist.

i would break myself into tiny tiny pieces and flip them over
to show you even when shattered i am but a mosaic and you
are the artist.

tangled.

i found you
down there
amidst the clumsy
wire and plastic
hangers
tangled

you had no
business there
)i thought(

but
you loved the company
and now it's where
we reside.

you have the right to remain original.

you have the right to remain original.

full of grace that feeds my sin.

let it be known my soul fires up an undeniable blaze each time you speak. it's like you are full of grace that feeds my sin.

social security numbers.

they knew
)like the back
of their own
hands(
each others'
social security
numbers.

that is a love
in numeric order.

where love was first discovered.

i've sailed above the clouds
even visited the ninth one
and realized that you've
taken me further to places
much higher than where
clouds are formed. you,
my lover, are the spaceship
that blasts us off beyond
the planetary system
where love was
first discovered.

the gasps between each breath.

let me be
the gasps
between
each breath
so i
can feel
what it's like
for you
to catch yourself
and
so you
can know
i'm always there
in moments
you never thought
possible
for anyone
to exist.

i used to close my eyes under water.

i used to
close my eyes
under water
fearful to burn
them;
but with you
my dear water child
no matter how deep
or shallow
i will swim
under water
with my eyes
open.

love is a dedication page.

love is a dedication page
where the blinking cursor
visited before the book
was ever written
permanently placing
a line of poetry
and
plasters your name
so you will
forever live.

each day something beautiful happens.

each day something beautiful happens
seeing the rise of your cheekbones
in different angles sends tactical
goosebumps on secret missions
to the chambers of my heart.
the beauty of your face
isn't what holds my interest.
it's plotting out my own
special ops to see the glow
in your eyes triggered
by the lift of your cheeks
each day i see
something beautiful.
please excuse the lens
of mine eyes
as i capture
the curves of
your lips.

heartbeat trembling.

romance doesn't live in a box of delightful chocolates
nor does it occupy the petals of a floral arrangement
nay it lays dormant quiet still the color of it lingers
on a heartbeat trembling.

exotic expression.

i want
more than
you'll ever know
to be that
expression
on your face
that one
you do so well
yes. that very one.
where you
try to hold back
that smile
when i say something
whatever it may be
that you have
an answer to
but instead
you smirk
and resist
the urge
to respond
leaving me
forever enjoying
that exotic
expression
on your face
one i hope to be
if you let me.

in the dark.

i sleep
not because
i'm tired
but because
you
are
my eyelids
and
when the
shades
are drawn
i
see you
better
in the
dark.

you breathe life.

i've made room for you next to me
next to the past that once accrued dust

you breathe life into what was once
spilled ink.

not just anyone can stand that much heat.

if,
hot temperatures
and pressure
form diamonds
then,
i
will be cool
and gentle
because
you
have been through
enough

to me
your shine
isn't
what makes
you beautiful
not just anyone
can stand
that much heat
and intensity
the way you did
and still do.

you always find a way.

filling this glass
with
countless
cubes of ice
followed by
a long
liquid pour
sends a
flirtacious sound
that
cracks and hisses
like an
aria
quenching my thirst.
it seems
you always
find a way
to infuse
your aura
even in
a cylindrical
mason jar.

i love you.

i love you
not for the words you say
but for the things you do.

the story of you.

the story of you
began long before
outstreched wings
tore through colorless air.

the story of you
is etched in stone
crafting new lines
like an aged oak
standing
the test of time.

the story of you
is stark with used bristles
on hand-crafted canvas
writhed in finger paint.

behold
the story of you
is a tale told best
near nature and art.

every bit of you.

you
are
an epidemic
that has
spread
like wildfire
there is no cure
and it's too late
addicted
and
smitten
by every
bit of you.

laughter is love.

laughter is love
busting at the seams
coming up for air.

burning point.

i burn for you
at a burning point
so hot
it melts away
all the
scared tendencies
i've collected
over the years.

airwaves.

my love for you
isn't the kind
that's televised.
it
in a word
is the
electric hum
a
static vibration
that you often
feel and hear
and never question
its presence
in a room.
my love
swarms in
like
warm embrace
on a cool
summer's day
more refreshing
than anything
broadcast on
television;
my love
is all of me
on airwaves
just for you.

amor on glass.

staring out this window
watching snow fall
wing-tipped ice spatters
on glass

it dances
it glides
with such grace

the bounce of sound
harmonizes the descent
as my sight becomes
cascaded with white
and my body temp
declines

you surround me

with innocent frozen raindrops
showcasing just one
of many ways
how you are always around

in the little things

my snow angel
amor
on glass.

you are magic.

you are magic
the kind that
hypnotizes
the soul
and pinpoints
broken bones
and detached sinew;
you
are
the benevolent spell
that scoops
up the pieces
making me
whole
again.

the souls way.

panic is the souls way of finding equilibrium
when it comes into contact with the perfect match.
love can feel like a heart attack
just breathe it all in.

why read a book on love.

why read a book on love
when the text is already
transcribed in your essence

let me sight read
and use my eyes
and hands

teach me

how to love you
like a book
never could.

love is.

love is
tension felt in a room
when
two newly acquainted souls
sit next to one another
anticipating
the first touch.

space between hands

become unbearable

and nerves make each

hold their breath

until inches
become millimeters

and distance soon breaches
territory unexplored.

i hold my breath
each and every time
our souls
intertwine.

inferno.

double tap
bare skin
with soft lips
and zoom in
close
close enough
to watch
how easy it is
to start
a fyer
a fier
a fyr
a fire.

only you
can cause
this inferno
with
a tuch
a tutch
a tutsh
a touch.

sorry if i stare.

coiled in the drop dead essence of all things you
i can't help but wonder)moreso marvel(at how
your eyes carry so much exuberance in a world
made beautiful with the perfumed breath and
subtle ways of an angelic creation. so sorry if
i stare. but resisting such a sunset goes against
my daily routine.

moments.

there are these
moments
where
i can't help but
scratch my head
as if
trying to think
of a line
title or random quote
and i get stuck
until i figure it out.

see. you
have that effect
on me
i swear
i swear
we've met before
i just can't
for the life of me
remember
in which lifetime
we first
crossed paths.

acoustic bliss.

you are acoustic bliss.
stripped down
your naked soul
dances
on guitar strings
all i see is stars.

water.

you are water
from fresh
rocky mountain rivers
that slithered
and palmed
my undeserving ocean

drinking you
fills all that i am:
i need you
to stay alive.

soak me up.

soak me up
absorb
all the
melanin
in my skin
i'd give you
all of my color
a palette
of the sun.

you blot the sky.

there are days
i cannot see the sun

there are nights
i cannot see the moon

you blot the sky
with a blink
and dissappear
before my eyes.

the echo of your heartbeat.

through wind chatter
flared tornadoes
hurricane showers
and tsunami tempests
the echo of your heartbeat
is a beautiful sign
that clear skies and
the curves of your face
are soon to be
in sight.

the honey on your bones.

my goodness
the honey on your bones
blushes through your skin.

searching.

i have yet to discover
a word. phrase. analogy.
worthy to be displayed
next to your name.
yet the three ice cubes
that fight for spots
in the whisky glass
sending chills of
70 proof affection
through each
honey caramel sip
a full body high
nostalgic tastes of you.

looking for aurora.

i'll spend a lifetime
the hymns of every sec
to uncover
stumble upon
bring forth
vivacious soliloquy
as dazzling as you.

forgetting to breathe.

"do you think of me all the time?"
you asked with a peak of sadness.

"i see you in everything:
even the slightest tilt of the clouds
remind me of how graceful you are.
like there is air beneath your feet
and you break the laws of gravity."

"is that so?" a hint of sun
clamored from your mouth.

"when i don't think of you
it's like forgetting to breathe."

sky love.

sky love
is the best love
it has no end
and even if
our temperature drops
and the weather changes
my love
is always there
in all
four seasons.

fine art.

you are watercolor seas
and latch-hook fields
painted skies and
hand sculpted dunes
treble clef winds
arched mountainsides
and poetic hills;
you are fine art.

i'll lay.

the writing process
is cruel and arduous
chaos declares war and
my mind is surrounded
by an infantry of words

sometimes
you have to lay in defeat
so your soul
can get what it needs

for you
i'll lay
i'll lay
i'll lay.

nothing fiction about you.

there is nothing fiction about you
my poetry shall be the bio
for all that you are
will be added to the dictionary
lined next to 'royalty'
stacked with 'nature'
across from 'elegant' and
neighbor to 'gift';
i never knew
all that you are
as you are
all these words
new to me.

euphoric bliss.

i opened up
i let you in
and ever since
euphoric bliss.

definition.

giver.
noun

one who gives with every once of their soul
and inspires others to do the same.

"giver is the word that best describes you."

tragedy.

tragedy darkens your eyes
it's visible in each blackened pupil
you've adjusted to the pain
when the first time shouldn't have happened
blaming yourself when you aren't the problem
makes this travesty more tragic
find strength and courage
when it comes to your story
they said you couldn't shouldn't won't
think to live
  lead your own life
time to show them otherwise
turn this tragedy into an epic journey
so hold tight to your pen
and don't dare let another
  write for you again.

an odd prayer.

circles smaller
connections deeper
brings close those meant to be nearer
not in distance or proximity
instill in us a desire to care
an odd prayer
  solemn request
i plead you listen.

they want it all from you.

they want it all from you
and will suck until dry
careful selection necessary
)to whom you give your adoration(
i love you too much
or i'd keep my mouth shut
another waste of that loving energy
on the heart of a two-bit hustler.

russian roulette.

russian roulette
such a dangerous game
'specially when lovers sit
on opposite ends of the table

who will go first

this pretense of bravey
playing with a loaded gun
each squeeze on the trigger
to get a rise from the other
rigged is this illusion
that no one will get hurt

keep gambling with the heart
die slowly be torn apart.

on my lips i carry your name.

on my lips i carry your name
through me you always live
ready for our next adventure
will love you even after forever's end.

magic heartbeats.

here's to love. life. happiness.

may we be who we want
express how we feel
deliver our words
like magic heartbeats

so let it be written
so let it be done.

cosmic rendezvous.

tonight's sky held a beautiful view
the moon so grey. a shadowy hue
mine eyes wouldn't avert
the sun peaked behind
leaving a bottom crescent shine
i couldn't take a picture
)no i did not dare(
that cosmic rendezvous
will stay with me
it was breathtaking
reminded me of you.

waiting for your return.

missing you
is rain to the window
drips of melancholy
subside
at the dawning of sun
yet i still love the rain
waiting for your return.

admire just admire.

from the chill in the air
i knew it would snow
hoped for a downpour
some snow glow affair
all i really wanted
)deep down inside(
was to see
the footprints
you'd leave
and admire
just
admire.

favorite wrinkle.

each crack
holds a story
the braille on the wall
valleyed depths so different
it takes patience
but i mission
to scale them all
starting with
my favorite wrinkle
on your skin.

ode to you.

i see myself vividly through words
mirrors unnecessary i can read the difference
between what was and what is

the past i accept what you taught me
long nights and sleepless hours enlightened my insights

i've made it to one side from another
using the same words with clearer meaning
tunnel visioned definition

the soul in this body
niched in alphabetic muse
sails the curve of every word

ode to you.

crème glacée.

not sure why
and i never question it
i let the ice cream sit
on the cold metal spoon
and i wait
for the exact moment
and not a moment too soon
for the perfect drop to melt
to drink into your mouth
such a science to it
my homemade vanilla
crème glacée.

take life as it comes.

hearing love in your voice
an indescribable tone
drowned the terminal illness and
suffocated the pain
i've known you forever
tho it just took a day
'take like as it comes'
wise council you gave me
i hold those words dearly
)clenched tight to my chest(
looking forward seeing
that beautiful louisiana smile
and your salt-n-pepper hair
some day again
some day again.

for grandpa larry

the masks we wear.

maybe
just maybe
the masks
we wear
will become
transparent cloaks
so that
our caged souls
finally can see
once and for all
what we hide it from
maybe
just maybe
our souls
will breathe.

fixated light.

art isn't
the object
three-dimensional
in plain view
but the reflection
on the wall
spattered
in angular black
from ambient light
shaping a well-rounded
slanted perspective
of you

i
the fixated light
to expose
your
truth.

what if what if.

what if
what if
i were clay
and
your hands
your hands
crafted
my
soul.

i see you.

i see you
in the leaves
of all shades
i just hope
that
if a strong wind
gusts you away
the buds
you leave
behind
will
blossom
in the nature
we planted
no matter
the season.

love currency.

i'll
spend
all
of
my
cents
to
carousel
with
you
all
over
the
world
just
accept
my
love
currency
as
checks.

flirting eyes.

flirting eyes
seek truth;
oh what they
find.

tiles.

we are but tiles jigsawed together.
what binds us?
grey matter—
a gunked ravine
that catches
excess waste
that spills over
from one to the other—
your tiles
are what keep mine
)from coming undone(
and i will shine your surface
taking night watch
in admiration
of each piece of you
that sticks
to me.

don't flee.

your legs
have done enough
running
pace through
problems
don't flee.

north star.

you never know
how bad your eyes are
until you find the north star
she'll guide you
you'll find that what you
thought you saw
wasn't really seeing
at all.

becoming my gravity.

the cold air
fills empty space
whirls every particle
and the winds
in a gentle manner
transport a lovely
fragrance
lo lo
see how it
collects
your vibrant
savoir faire
floats
becoming
my gravity.

the hare has always been me.

it's tiring—
running after awhile—
i'd imagine
even more
cumbersome
when tortouise thoughts
catch up;
the hare
has always
been me.

insatiable.

wants become a thirst unquenchable
be temporate with desire or thirst infinitely.

fingerprints on my soul.

each time the light flickers off
i no longer am afraid of the dark
my eyes adjust quickly
i collect my bearings
and realize
it is the black fog hue
that showcases
all of your fingerprints
on my soul.

you bewitched the world.

you bewitched the world
with your cat eyes and
feline sway
the purr of your existence
the growl of your power
the meow of your desire
the hiss of your beauty
make some fearful and
jealousy unjustly judges you
but nothing could ever
ever ever ever
break your spirit
for you are too strong
and too agile and
too quick and too
intelligent to heed
nonsense.

everything about you.

everything falls into place
everything happens in time
everything is meant to be

you were crafted with
planetary instruments
birthed under the stars
the ground moves
in tune to your footsteps

everything about you
was stenciled on a blueprint
seek and ye shall find
destined to be great.

the key ingredient.

they may take your idea
try to make it their own
they'll never have your spirit
that's the key ingredient.

bring back our girls.

i don't have a daughter
but i pray if someday i shall
if she were ripped
from my sight
and taken
the equilibrium of my body
would earthquake
and sprial into a frenzy;
may they be found
the lost daughters
of our motherland
bring back our girls
bring back their smiles.

for nigeria

you broke my levees.

you broke my levees
flooded dry lands
submerged every open wound
and your annointed waters
replenished my soul.

compliments.

compliments
)words full of butterflies(
richochet on two-way mirrors
glass that speaks truth
i just hope the images
you catch
surpass the subconscious level
and exhale before your eyes
so you
can see
what i see.

the shoes in the corner.

the shoes in the corner
how they flail and hold space
you aren't even home
but i feel you
honey scented laces and
old mud you tracked in
time before last

there they stand
flopped over in the corner
until you wear them again
my sweet home decor.

i can't give you flowers.

i can't give you flowers.
the kingdom of what inhabits unsaid temperament
wants to hike miles. forge mountains. etch tablets.
write songs. mold sculptures. manipulate clouds.
travel to the moon. catapult through time. traverse
the great pyramids. to tell you:
thank you.
for pricking. stomping. holding
the essence of this god-like manifestation
residing in my being.
i can't give you flowers
that soon will wither under the tuscan sun
i can't give you flowers
that adequately opens up that space you've held for me
so i cannot wait)not another minute(
this is the beginning to reveal and blossom the seeds
and plant them all around

i am
we are
the abundance of watered ripples
waves that shall collapse upon eachother
let the bowels of these words bud in your soul
tunnel down deep to the chambers of your heart
and wedge an imprint to travel with you
)wherever you go(
i can't give you flowers
not one petal. stem. or leaf.
without extending my thanks.

breathing you in.

i love how the wind
trails behind you
as if servant to your soul
you cut through life
and the air sends
the perfume of you
to be absorbed
by all living things
i can't but help
breathing you in.

making you ring.

vintage
like a rotary phone
i pocket your skin
dialing soft spots
winding ten digits
just to reach you
all in all
the bells i hear
before we connect
is an appetizer
a la mode:
i love
making you ring.

love territory.

my soul is unraveled
)once it was coiled and lost(
a wanderer of time and space
i venture for light-filled place
a radiance surpassing description
come along with me
let's ride the horizon
discover each other
in love territory and
forget which soul
belongs to which.

will you be my.

will you be my _____?

circle
yes   no   maybe

handwritten
love notes
folded
and folded again—
what will be the answer
should have
attached a pen;
no matter
no matter
put yourself out there
may the odds
be in your
favor.

in a gallery on display.

in a gallery on display
i could see you on sante fe
but the majestic texture
of each outline
that shapes the canvas of you
was meant to be filled
with love and light
free from static living
it is we
with fortunate luck
who aspire to live
and be viewed
on your walls

starstuck
by the very thought
of you
and your lovely outline
walking by my potrait.

on a crusade for words.

on a crusade for words
to sound out
to feel out
to love out
all the things you are
still haven't found
what i'm
feeling for.

i see time by looking into your eyes.

all the tiny little
pebbles
in the big large
hour glass
no longer
measures time
i've knocked it
to its side
writing our name
in stagnant sand
to make use
of our forever
together;
objects
tracking
ticks and tocks
can be
of better use—
i'd rather not
worry
how long or
short
the hour;
i see time
by looking
into
your
eyes.

stargazing.

i star gazed
searching
the pitch-black
galaxy
even crafted
)no crafstman am i(
miles of lasso
with me eyes.
i saw one
in its own world—
in blistered awe
eye blinked
destroying me lasso.
now
i simply stare
in your stars
direction
hoping
and
wishing
i catch
your attention;
turns out
you were the one
stargazing
hoping
and
wishing
for my
affection.

for the one who is kind is beautiful.

selfless
is the soul
who cares;
for the one
who is
kind
is
beautiful.

you are you.

you are you
and no one
no one
no one
no one
does that better
than you
even
the stench
of you
is a fragrance
others merely
wish
they could
bottle and dab
on each
wrist.

like braille.

wrinkles
o how they
speak for themselves

as we grow older
and
elasticity is lost

my hands
o how they
will be used

to read
your skin
like braille.

your accent.

your accent
is a strummed harp
and i am
infatuated.

your love is magic i believe in.

neverland
was a child's
dream
that always
fascinated me.
not the actual place
but the pixie dust
all sparkly and golden
)the magic it bestowed(
happy thoughts
and a spritz of
fairy splendor
would cast us
to new heights
if
we only believed;
i fly higher
than one could
ever imagine
and
your love is magic
that i believe in.

before you or i ever existed.

i've waited
before you
or i
ever existed
just to
stand in line
and feel
tender wind
brush by and
comandeer
your every look;
seeing you
is my world
on a ferris wheel
and we
and we
have this
park of amusement
to ourselves.

passport kisses.

this 3 x 5
passport
is riddled
with
your
kisses;
the best part
about traveling
if when you
stamp
a new page.

midnight moon.

day grew thin
and fell upon itself
like a
thimble on its side
and as the hours
whimpered and groaned
i saved enough
drops of energy
to blow you a kiss
sending a shockwave
adding yet another
dimple
on your surface
my midnight moon.

an imperfect host.

can you see me?
i floated away
from my body
and observed.
so this
is what i look like?
translucent light
spat in disjointed
angles.
yes. i see you.
can you stop
staring.
in a moment
of reflection
i
left my self
spoke
in third person
and saw
)for the first time(
what my soul
needed to see.
an imperfect host.

;.

this ongoing war
involving two
independent clauses
was crafted on pyramids
calculated using the stars;
we are
but static sentences
searching for a bond
;
such an electronic charge
it's a moon
dropping a line
fishing
for a sun.

everything to you is a fire.

everything to you is a fire
you told me once. it is. it is.
i don't want our flame our love
our embers to ever ever go out.

look at me look at you.

promise me
promise me
you'll always
look at me
look at me

look at you
look at you
i'll always
promise you
promise you.

the octaves of your voice.

music seeps into my soul
like a travelling harmonic tour
inside deep deep inside
and the cruel textured lyrics
stab me all over all over
the baseline bumps
my body can't help but move;
how is it
how is it
possible
the octaves of your voice
tranquilizes my spirit.

nostalgic souls.

these trail of words will lead us back to each instance. back to each happenstance. back to each eye glance. back to each beautiful fatal moment. when our nostalgic souls dance to the rhythm of a lifetime of happiness and recall the how the when the what and whys of being condemned to love each other. a ravishing breadcrumb tale.

love is light.

love is light
creeping at windows daybreak
release the shade
illuminate your life
and watch the sun rise
it's the radiance alone that's
strong enough
worthy enough
curious enough
to give love
a chance.

don't put out the light.

you
are
an everlasting
flame
staying lit
through
any weather
a lighthouse
in
all
chaos
i seek
your glow
heat and
smoke;
don't
)i beg of you(
put out the light
don't put out the light.

love magic.

like a spark plug
you ignite my soul
sending super-sonic
wavelengths of electricity
hardwiring every little detail
energizing each heartbeat
causing uncontrollable
smirks and smiles.
you must have love magic
that fires up air and gas
shooting silent sparks
that dance on the epidermis
and melt.

tenderness to mend a broken heart.

do we all deserve love. asked the one with many fears. yes. we do. responded the other and wiped those fears away. sometimes when we speak all we are asking for all that we really need is tenderness to mend a broken heart.

this love thing.

in the blink
of an eye
it can happen
)faster than
you would ever
think(
this love thing
will lay dormant
sleep still
and bleed out
when you least
expect it.

why this infatuation with the stars. the moon. the sun.

why this infatuation with the stars. the moon. the sun.

those
are smoke signals
a warning
that you're
near

the sky
a beacon
i gravitate and
wander
towards
all things
that
cosmically
remind me
of you.

you aren't broken.

you aren't broken
and your bones aren't delicate
the only fracture
is the break between your lips
and if you will it
the space between air and sound
will let you in
and all you may need
is to be listened to.
you have saved yourself
far too many times.
not everyone
needs rescuing.

worry worry.

worry worry
the natural reaction
when your
heart skips a beat
after encountering
the perfect sunrise
and you are sent
into outer space
with a magic kiss.
worry worry
worry no more
it is not worry at all
you're in love
you're in love.

you have consumed my soul.

you have consumed my soul
and tangoed with it
quick
quick
slow
i never had a chance.

being with you.

being with you
is like
living close
)extremely close(
to the equator.
you divide me
into two
hemispheres
and balance
my darkness
and my
light.

the pull of you.

in you everything sank
and the pull of you
is equal to that of the moon.
i am a body of water
whose tides can't help
but be attracted)like magnets(
rising and falling
in your presence or absence.

after pablo neruda

give me nothing.

give me nothing.
i already have enough.
you are my everything
a gift i unwrap
day in and day out.

the sum of all of you.

i will share
all that i am
plastering
penned ink
not wasting
any of its
spatter.
all that i am
is the sum
of all of you
and the winds
will carry
these words
until the end
of time
and all that
remains
will be
blotted stains
of us.

i have studied your lips.

i have studied your lips
every line. dip. and bend.
and
have come to realize
one truth.
the way you move
is in perfect unison
with the perk
and pout
of your mouth
orating coded syllables
only i can make out.

make our own atmosphere.

i can't compete.
hell.
i'm not even
in the same
layer
as the sun
moon and stars
yet
if you
let me
i'll
take you past
pluto
and you and i
will make
our own
atmosphere.

your skin is a wonder of the world.

your skin is a wonder of the world.

love is a mountain.

love is a mountain
with no way around.
up and through
is the only option.
when you reach the summit
and stake your claim
the bumps and bruises
headaches and anguish
will be replaced with
sighs of relief
and tears of disbelief
in awe of part one
of a journey's end.
getting there is worth it.
getting there is worth it.
breathe it all in.
love.
your new oxygen
has been waiting
has been waiting
but
you'll never know
what you've
been missing
until you get there
so start the climb.
you must.

the universe belongs to you.

the universe
belongs to you
it's yours
it's yours
and
my one request
)a meager and selfish plea(
will you
can you
do you mind
drizzling your cosmic lights
like spring rain showers
airbrushed across the sky.
i beg for them.
hoping one of your stars
will fall within
my reach.

let the waters find their way.

your tears
o. how they
river dance
down
down
your ebon skin.
no.
do not
wipe away
let the waters
find their way
back
to where
they belong.

utter madness the things i'd do for you.

i would crawl
on fractured ground
after standing
with arms and eyes
flexed to the sky
pleading
for the sun
to always keep you warm.
utter madness
the things i'd do for you.

let me become these words.

let me become these words
sprawled on parchment and spread my ashes
past the margins
because i want to lay next to
every halfway stanza i've professed to you.
all that is left will be for my alphabetic soul
to kiss yours forever.

eclipse.

if you mind the gap
between my head and my heart
then you must stomach my sink holes.
if you withstand the ebbs and flows
of my moods then. and only then.
my dear our moons eclipse.

up close.

i see you in pixels
microscopic bits
cosmic wavelengths
others might like you
simply zoomed
all the way out
to see the perfect picture
clean and clear and crystal
not i
i prefer up close
blurred lines
jagged edges
undefined colors
to examine
the real you
below atomic-level
to lay with and
cherish
your
sediment
soul.

may there be more of you.

i believe in humanity
even when my bones quake
and shutter when i hear and see
devastation. you are a divine soul
and as your footsteps sail this dimension
of time i hunger for others to be as pure and
human as you. the kind that has a heart big enough.
words gentle enough. to extend i love you's as tears fall
from such a sincere vessel. may there be more of you. we
need you. and your pools of hope. don't give up on us. don't
give up on me.

shake.

you paralyze my entire soul.
no words no sound no movement.
you are so powerful. i shake
when we kiss.

back to life.

if looks could kill
i've died a thousand times
and you
you bring me
back to life.

the bubbles we make.

i hold my breath
to keep from drowning.
your love is like deep sea diving.
and it is you that reminds me
to inhale slow and steady.
taking your air in
and loving you
all the way out.
i love
the bubbles
we make.

en la distancia.

you are a short film.
the slow-motion
dramatic
romantic
black and white classic
fleeting melodic
i-hope-we-make-it
tear jerking musical anthem
never ending story.
i just hope to be
in the ending credits
scrolling
next to you
hand-in-hand
fading
en la distancia.

worth losing track of.

a dream vacation
is hiding cellular devices
and misplacing clocks
inching close to your face
so that the distance
between your mouth
and my mouth
are equidistant
to that of our hands
and as the earth rotates
our paradise is filled with
sign language
and chemistry experiments
where
sunsets and white sand
waterfalls and moon showers
don't come close
)not even worth the compare(
to your smile and your laughter.
that's the first wonder
of my world worth
losing track of.

on my walk home.

on my walk home
i only heard
the click clack
of my shoes
)an all too familiar sound(
but on this night
the vibration of concrete
harmonized
with the twinkling stars
and the pounding of pavement
served as the instrumental soundtrack
that crescendoed
when i opened the door
and fell
into your arms.

a note to you.

we haven't spoken in a while
and i'm not quite sure where to begin
but
i wanted to sit and reflect
in quiet stillness
and enjoy your company.
be proud of all the things you've done
and have yet to accomplish
these training days
are but the ground work
for what is to come.
do the things
your heart desires
and know for a fact
without shadow of doubt
that you are
where you need to be
and i brag about you
because there's so much
greatness in you.
i honor. respect.
and salute you.

if i had one word left to say.

if i had one word
left to say
let me live in silence
until that fateful day
when all i have
built up and mustered
vibrates from my vocal chords
and escapes passed my lips
after i've seen
and seen again and again
the lift of your walk
the twist of your hips
the sway of your shoulders
the curl of your hair
the movement of your mouth
then and only then
will i let my final word rest.

freckles.

freckles
are
beauty marks
so
simple
so
endearing
i
fall in love
all
over
again
each time
i find
another
on your
skin.

the forever hello.

you are the forever hello
lodged in my ribcage.
may you always know
you have a home
in my heart.

they don't know poetry.

whoever says you aren't poetry
doesn't know poetry.
that's all i will say
about their imagination.

but back to you
)always back to you(

when you look up
when you look down
when you look around
all in your presence
the world is brighter
vibrantmore
filledmore
lovedmore
wateredmore

you bring with you
such
such
such
such
light
)more than light(
light before light
evolved
into what it is now
that is poetry.
you are poetry.

thank you for us.

not a day goes by without me searching for you. turning towards you. wandering in your direction. to get my gravity. to find my balance. to find my true north. sometimes anxiety creeps in if when i look and there is no proof you are near. no proof you are on your way back. no proof you cast your magic into the sky like flare like house of hearts like i need you like water for chocolate. like river needs bend. like solar needs stars like you greet the lost who become found embraced by your system by your orbit by your galaxy that oxygen needs most to exist i'm losing my breath. did you catch it. this is what loving you is like. not wanting to pause so not to miss a beat)your beat(to soundtrack the steps of life so not to say i blinked and lost sight of your scent there i go again not breathing you do that like living under water there are pockets that pocket fresh air that you can take under there instead of going up to surface but your surface is never in the shallow end it's at the bottom where i lent you)gave you(my heart)this heart(i love you love. for letting me in your ocean. for letting me see your planetarium. for letting me near your energy. for letting me. me. how rare is that. how rare are you. the best kind. most wonderful kind. the space of us doesn't have to be verified or applauded by or understood by or certified by or approved by anyone but us. but us. but us. but us. but you are the reason there is an us. thank you for us. for growing us. for thinking us. for futuring us. for investing us. for centering us. for reminding us. for mining us. there is gold in us because you lend yours to us. not a day goes by without me searching for you. turning towards you. wandering in your direction. finding you is finding me. love is where you are love. love is where you are love.

the greatest rays.

who needs the sun
when your eyes)your eyes(
are the greatest rays
that warm
my soul.

never had the courage but i do now.

back then. when then was beginning. before then turned into always. i knew. i knew)i always knew(you would be the last time i'd fall and keep falling and keep falling and keep falling and keep falling and i knew i loved you before i had the courage to tell you. perhaps saying it before the right moment the right tempo the right way would make it real and vanish as if it never happened. was it too good were we too good was it like the others)could never be like the others(soon it would get hard and running away was the easiest charge to the heart instead of breaking it apart. you saved me. i remember saying that in my mind over and over and over and over from a path not meant for me but i was headed because i didn't know better. you showed me a world i knew existed but didn't think it was a world for people like me. you saved my life. i would say out loud. and fall into those words as if you needed saving too. but you didn't. you were and still are the greatest present manifested.

smiling looks good on you.

smiling looks good on you.

the lover in me honors the lover in you.

within you there is more. always more. deeper more. beyond more. beautifully more. and without having to say more or probe more or reach more all i want to all i need to all i have to extend your way is a saying. is a sounding. is an affirming. a language. a vibrating pulse that captures the everything of you. that whispers i see you and i love you and i never get it right i never say it how it truly feels just witnessing your light. to witness you from this vantage point is the greatest cherishing i may ever experience in this chapter you so graciously allowed me to visit some of your pages in. this life you grant me window into probably has so many handprints and words left unsaid on the sill so when you catch this please know this is my amateur way of collecting every unsaid unsaid in hopes to download all at once when it reaches your soul in one word in one breath in one second i plan to unveil it and pass it on to you i pray it finds you where you are and sees you where you are and lifts you where you are and welcomes you where you are how you always see and lift and welcome me like every day is homecoming. like every day is a holy day. like every day is especially made with me in heart. how you do that i do not know i do not question that big space you grant me and i thank you quietly and i want to thank you loudly so you hear it echo all around you and fill in all the buckets all the gaps all the in-between where everyone even me has fallen short for you love. are you ready love. how can anyone ever find a string of light to treasure you the way you deserve to be treasured. how can anyone be as you are to every being. how can anything get to the level get to the depth get to the temperature get to the summit without losing their breath on their way to you. this is my try. this is my attempt. this is my water approaching your ocean. dearest one. it may not be enough)never enough for your fullness(but i found these roses for you: lovasté. the lover in me honors the lover in you.

piece in peace.

if you're tired it's all good. i'll be here regardless.
in no rush for you to recoup for you to energize
for you to push to something that time can wait
longer for. peace to all your pieces healing.
piece in peace. and if you need me know
i am not going anywhere. staying.
on standby. nearby. same place.
some room. across miles
and miles wherever you are.
if you need me gone i will go.
to give you space as much as little.
to give you love as much as little.
always double your need is what i prepare
cause there is there no matter how you present it.
your heart is priority priority so rest so rest.

our title don't matter.

call us whatever. so long as we're together. don't care the name what matters is our feeling. whatever you want us to be we will be. my heart is yours been that way since forever.

lost and found.

we weren't really looking. perhaps one of us was. but no mistake was made when we met and caught each other by surprise. not much can be done when what is meant to happen catches up with you. you never know you are lost until a void gets filled when you see what your eyes have been correcting for but the prescription had never been filled. not much can be done the moment two suns became one and from that point on everything just gets brighter and brighter and takes on a life of its own.

lift me to your atmosphere.

what it would be like to be a cloud how they puff about
floating slow none more powerful than the other
roaming free. you are those frozen crystals
nestled neatly in the sky. soft. gentle.
a work of art. lift me to your atmosphere
so i can embrace liquid droplets
and be a cloud just like you.

mighty sol.

the sun shines
when you're away
it's like
the further you travel
the sun comes closer
as if
a memorandum
of understanding exists
to keep me warm
so you won't be missed;
you
are a mighty sol.

burst like a butterfly from its cocoon.

i feel i could burst
like a butterfly
from its cocoon
spread these limbs
take flight
and jump
out of this skin
into yours
and explode
becoming one.
even at an atomic level
you radiate matter
and i hope
my negative
and your positive
particles
beautifully mate.

the vows we never wrote.

waking up to you in early mornings and late at nights is one of the reasons i look forward to saying i do. because committing to that and the in-betweens the peaks and the valleys and the staying when it is bound to flame and scorch and my feet will want to flee is worth remembering our humble hearted beginning. to you i declare my all my every my person for you i will show always my true self amidst a world that will never understand me. to you i give the deepest parts i have yet to find and together whatever you find is yours)always yours(because you'll be the one encouraging me to go down go down go down with held breath knotted stomach with you by my side in spirit or in person is the there i want to be for you too. for the no matter what's. for the in this together's. for the us against everyone else. to you i pledge to see you)always see you(when you yourself go unseen. when you yourself dark and storm and think you're no longer beautiful)you'll always be beautiful(. to you it is us it is our is it we who decide where the going is where the growing is where the hoping is where the loving is and that is wherever you are love. wherever you are love. you say things like i am something special but it is you who are the greatest specialty the greatest unearthing the greatest treasure every discovered and yet there is so much more of you yet to be fully discovered as there are parts of you you haven't set sail towards. and that excites me. you ignite me. you inspire me. you better me. in all the ways i can't do anything but dedicate my life to appreciate you for. to care for you more than i cared for you the day before will be my mission my task my honor to love you better and better forever and ever. to you and the crowns should we ever raise any will have the most beautiful someone watering them and adding jewels in their soil. you are my living duty my reason for being. to love every part of you choosing you daily to love you deeply always always always. i do. i always did.

i'll never play for your heart.

i'll never play for your heart
but i'll meet you at half court
and to you i'll dedicate
each shot.

xo.lvst.

you never know. you never know. when it's your time. so i hope you gasp for it as if there is none left. not in desperation but in pursuit of every moment making it meaningful. making it memorable. making it worthy of any energy you give it. so in the last breath between your hands may these words guide you how you always guide the ones who know you and the ones who want so badly to get to know more of you. to create the life you desire to lead and live. to push down what fears you and experience joy like no other. experience love like no other. experience you like no other. and connect with parts of yourself that have yet to be introduced to you. chapter and page and bookmark every chance as your chance to inhale doubt and turn it into gold. it is your magic that is stopping you)don't let your magic stop you(visit it more visit you more tap into it more release it more. your magic isn't to be tamed or accessed by anyone you don't want access granted to. you. oh you. incredible you. the xo that gifts every space you grace. the lvst that ignites heartbeats. when i say xo i mean i feel you. i see you. i appreciate you. i acknowledge you. i water you. when i say lvst i mean i love you. i honor you. i lift you. i admire you. all of you. infinitely you. no matter the season. no matter the change in weather. no matter the battles you seemingly face alone and have yet to tell a soul. i am here beloved. wholeheartedly beloved. because you never know. you never know. when it's your time. and i want to use every inch that exists between us and explore all the crevices. dive into the pours with wonder and not worry what we find but allow our wandering to wash over us in love love. you are my everything love. i don't say this enough love so maybe this volume will be talisman love. to flip to to hold to to break to to vow to and re-commit to. you create a calm in me that i wish i could return. receive this collection as mantra as affirmation as testimony for all the times you made me whole. made me better. this is for you. this is always for you. xo. lvst.

words can never come to an end they just blur into action into feeling into the ether where love just boomerangs back to look different impact different fill different. whether one line or no line struck your core perhaps you were inspired to love yourself or someone else harder as love is the shortest distance between souls the greatest antidote everyone deserves. the lover in me honors the lover in you. *lvst. xo. adrian michael*

i appreciate you 🌹